The Kontum Madonna

The Kontum Madonna

A collection of Viet Nam War poems

Poems by J. Vincent Hansen

with drawings
by Dick Adair

Illustrations are reproduced with the permission of Mrs. Dick Adair.

Some of these poems have been previously published under the title *Blessed are the Piecemakers* published by North Star Press of St. Cloud Inc.

First Edition

ISBN: 978-1-68201-121-8

North Star Press of St. Cloud Inc.
www.northstarpress.com

To Pappy:
who sat with me
on the wall

and

To Jeanette:
for doing what
all the King's horses
and all the King's men
could not.

A well-equipped soldier
carries with him the prayer
for some of his enemy to get away
to keep alive the ones who didn't.

JVH

Part i

"All pomp and pageantry on ready view–the grounds
lay thick with weapons, dark with flags."

The Tale of Kieu
Nguyen Du

A STORY

Once upon a time
in a far away land
of lute and lotus,
before they had a chance
to seed themselves,
I filled
an olive-drab vase
with Asian flowers–

now
only the barren places
remain.

THE WEDDING
OF TOMORROW AND SORROW

While War
can always be counted on
to trumpet the birth of Anger
and the death of Patience,
do not look for it
to announce the wedding
of Tomorrow and Sorrow.

SUNDRY THEOLOGY

Should someone ask
I will tell them

Viet Nam was that place
where:

a Hershey bar was worth
   five cigarettes

a pecan nut roll was worth
   five cans of ham and lima beans

a human life was worth
   nothing.

PUTTING BY FODDER
IN THE SILO OF EMPIRE

Mr. Brennan spent a whole semester
  on the Civil War–
had little blue and gray soldiers
  on an old library table
  front and center
  going round and round
  like wildebeests
  with worms in their brains–
had smaller battles going
  on windowsills–
Vicksburg
  on an olive drab filing cabinet
  in the corner–
Appomattox on a radiator
  by the window–
made it panoramic, spectacular,
  bigger than life–
had us believing
  there was more to war
  than Cain and Abel,
  more to war
  than grown men
  peeing on themselves
  at river crossings–

had us believing
  there was more.

CAESAR

He is
bold and blatant,
as well raw power
can afford to be.

But lo!

He is subtle too,
like when he wills
to disconnect a heart
and summons
a barber.

A FOREIGN POLICY

We turn
  His "Good News"
  into a ledger,

then put
  our sons
  on the line,

the front line
  to protect
  the bottom line.

SERGEANT ROYSTER
MEETS PRIVATE STANLEY

Sergeant Royster said:
  "Kill the rabbit, Private."
Private Stanley replied:
  "I cannot kill the rabbit, Sergeant."
Sergeant Royster repeated:
  "Kill the rabbit, Private."
Private Stanley replied:
  "I cannot kill the rabbit, Sergeant."
Sergeant Royster advised:
  "I am giving you a direct order, Private.
  Kill the rabbit."
Private Stanley replied:
  "I will not kill the rabbit, Sergeant."
Sergeant Royster persisted:
  "It would behoove you
  to kill the rabbit ASAP, Private."
Private Stanley replied:
  "I will not kill the rabbit, Sergeant."
Sergeant Royster bellowed:
  "Why won't you kill the damn rabbit, Private?"
Private Stanley replied:
  "Because it is wrong to kill, Sergeant."
Sergeant Royster shouted: "Wrong to kill?
  Then what in God's name are you doing
  in this man's army, Private?"
Private Stanley replied:
  "Nothing in His name, Sergeant."

After six months of side sink, Private Stanley was discharged with
what was called a personality disorder. (ie, He would not kill.)

Sergeant Eggers would begin his class by biting the head off a chicken. Then he would smile and say: "Good morning, men. My name is Sergeant Eggers and I'm a Ranger."

Jungle Warfare Training
Phan Rang, South Viet Nam

SERGEANT EGGERS

Spitting speckled feathers
Sergeant Eggers said for how
it would behoove us to pay attention,
he was going to teach us
how to drive a nose into a brain.

I looked down
at the thrashing White Sussex
at his booted feet–

then gazed beyond him
into the green hills
surrounding Phan Rang
and wished for another way
to get Diane Rossman's attention.

WHO?

Sergeant Klein
said: "Wasting a *gook*
is the biggest thrill
you'll ever get
with your pants on."

We
laughed
and
laughed
and laughed.

How we laughed.

Who were we then?

OH, LORD, MAKE IT LAST

Victor Charles, Mr. Two Steps, Delta Don,
Willie Peter, Daisy Cutter, Mama san–

Widow Maker, Wheeler Dealer, Harlem Hare,
Dragon Lady, Bouncing Betty, Papa Bear.

> What a production. What a cast.
> Oh, Lord, make it last!

Master Blaster, B.J. Bopper, G.I. Joe,
Jungle Pimp, Hanoi Hannah, Uncle Ho–

P.L. Panther, Jolly Roger, Johnny Reb,
Wrecking Ball, Hyper Sniper, Spider Webb.

> What a production. What a cast.
> Oh, Lord, make it last!

> Oh, Lord, make it last!

WE TAKE HIM ALONG

We take Him along–
this "7 times 70" God,
this "Love your enemy" God,
this "Thou shall not kill" God,
we take Him along.

Turn Him
from a breaking-bread God
into a breaking-starch God,
from a "turn the other cheek" God,
into a "MAKE MY DAY" God
and take Him along.

Make Him fall in–
make Him salute–
make Him march–
make Him shoot–
this "Thou shall not kill" God
and take Him along.

Your Left, Your Left,
Your Left, Right, Left.
Your Left, Your Left,
Your Left, Right, Left…

A MASQUERADE

Rifles slung,
laden with ammo,
we went as lovers:

lovers of democracy,
lovers of freedom,
lovers of peace.

We went as lovers:
"parry right and hold" lovers,
"rear take down and strangle" lovers,
"halt, or I'll blow your damn head off"
lovers.

Rifles slung,
laden with ammo,
we went as lovers.

VIRGIL

Above a chorus of frogs,
Virgil asked me if I knew where babies come from.
Then, without waiting for my answer,
he shared with me in the voice of secrets
that "babies come out from between
the breasts of a woman.
Did you know that Gunner?" he asked.
"Did you know that's how babies got here?"

Sensing how thick the air was with solemnity then,
I said: "Heck, Virgil. I know that. Everybody knows
that."

On the shelf that holds
the higher things that I have done in my life,
is that on the following morning
I did not share Virgil's notion–

for three days later Virgil was dead
and I still wonder
what way the sniper had of knowing
the one among us most out of place.

I wonder too, how much better equipped
I would be to recognize innocence now
had I been able to see more of Virgil's face that night–

more than a stingy moon and a Lucky Strike
had agreed on to show me.

THAT BIG BAND SOUND

Ace on B-52,
Daisy-Cutter on Cobra,
The Duke on Mortar,

Cannon Lawyer on artillery,
Spider Webb on claymore,
Jungle Pimp on grenades,

Widow Maker on M-60 machine gun,
Harlem Hare on M-16 rifle,
Papa Bear on M-45 pistol,

Hi-Fidelity on M-79 grenade launcher,
Hawkeye on M-14 rifle (with scope,)
Remington Raider filling in on M-50
machine gun,

when we were all on,
  we brought the house down;
  left 'em dead in the aisles.

18

SOLDIER

You see him
with rifle and bayonet
and say: "He is angry."

But I say:
"There is no anger in him."

You see
the plump grenades
hanging like dark fruit
from his chest
and say: "Surely
he is filled with hate."

I say:
"He knows not hate."

You say:
"He looks scared."

I say:
"Perhaps he is afraid."

You ask:
"What is it he fears?"

I say:
"Being alone."

A PINCH OF SALT

To
    lethal lieutenants,
    ambitious captains,
    and mad majors,

I add
    callous colonels,
    gung-ho generals,
    hard-boiled sergeants,
    and cocksure privates.

I mix in
    a duce-and-a-half
    of pre-sweetened Kool-Aid,
    some wait-a-minute vines,
    some betel nuts,
    some rice wine,
    and a small nun
    with a Baltimore Catechism.

I stir and stir and stir.

    The poems
    always set up confessional.

1965

In eight short weeks
Elmer went from
barn to barracks,
from altar boy
to ammo bearer,
and in the course
of the following year
killed seven people.

It was never so much
that he said *yes* to murder
as it was
he was unable to say *no*

to the way it was
in 1965.

WHEN

Viet Nam was when
darkness covered the earth
and the oft-sighted light
at the end of the tunnel
was nothing more
than a blazing Buddhist monk.

23

PART II

"Heaven gives weal or woe." the preacher said,
"yet from the human heart it also springs.
As heaven shapes our fate we lend a hand."

The Tale of Kieu
Nguyen Du

MANIFEST DESTINY

Harnessed
to
Myth and Illusion
like
powerful Percherons
in blinders,
we ploughed on,
never looking back
to see the blood
seeping
into
the furrow.

THE KONTUM MADONNA

All morning
we cheered from a nearby hill
as the planes softened the place
that we would go to in the afternoon–
      and we were happy.

The bombs exploding below
were like the sounds of a band
assigned to welcome us–
      and we were happy.

When we advanced
onto the bald patch of earth,
we met no resistance–
      and we were happy.

Amidst the burned and half-buried bodies,
we came upon a sitting woman and child
soldered together now in their place.

Gawking, we walked by
our high-tech sculpture,
hoping never having to look back.

We were young then and we were happy,
but we were foolish too–

foolish enough to think
we could leave that woman and child behind.

DEALING DEATH

"We do more before breakfast..."
Army recruiting ad

While
inserting
an
Ace
of
Spades
into
the
cleavage
of
a
still
warm
body–

a
cock
crows

and
he
wonders . . .

"YES SIR, YES SIR,
THREE BAGS FULL"

Herman mistook
a team of LRRPs*
for a squad of NVA,*

let loose with
40 rounds of duplex
and the LAW,*

moved out to view
his first kills;
one from Arizona,
one from Alabama,
one from North Dakota.

*LRRP (Lurp)– Long Range Reconnaissance Patrol
*NVA– North Vietnamese Army
*LAW– Light Anti-tank Weapon

"MADE BY MATTEL"

He would not go on now
if these was real folks.
Real folks, that is, like he knew
back in Popple Creek–

folks like Elmer Johnson
and his wife Clara–
folks like Mat Harper
and his brother Ben.

No, these was not real folks.
These was bogus little folks,
gun-powder gray and rubbery
by the time he got to 'em.

He would not go on now
if these was real folks.
Real folks, that is, like he knew
back in Popple Creek.

WALLOWING
AT TUY HOA

It rained
day and night
for thirty-one days
at Tuy Hoa.

We were thankful
for the opportunity
it afforded us
to cry unnoticed.

A LOVE POEM

On a rainy night in Tuy Hoa
Elmer made a memory.

Following orders
Elmer tied the prisoner to a tree,
bound her small brown wrists
with the olive-drab laces
from his jungle boots.

On a rainy night in Tuy Hoa
Elmer made a memory:

made a memory
from fibers of remorse and regret–
a durable memory
and then commenced
to schlep it around for five decades.

On a rainy night in Tuy Hoa
Elmer made a memory.

In quest of sleep
he tells himself now,
that she was fluent in Love
and that she believed his eyes
when they spoke to assure her–

none of this was his idea.

AN OLD MAN AND HIS CHICKENS

We killed
his chickens,
drank his
rice wine.

We did not
eat his chickens,
just killed
his chickens.

We had brought
our own chicken
in little
green cans.

UPON ENTERING
A MONTAGNARD HAMLET

The things we found
were simple things–
simple things
of wood and stone,
reed and earth.

Neither covered with chrome,
nor could they be plugged in;
we left them
strewn and smoldering
in our wake.

We were Americans first then,
soldiers second–

Americans first,
on our linear way from Wounded Knee
to only God knows where.

FAMILY

They laid now
in their shallow grave
like peasants that had fallen
onto Breugel's canvass
after a night of debauchery–

laid with their limbs
at the odd angles
that only a world *out of order*
can arrange.

Their calloused hands and splayed feet
determined to testify yet
on behalf of these little brown people
and their small patch of red earth.

The smells of gun powder and manure,
bloat and bile,
all blared now in unison of our blunder.

Not until later that night
would I realize it was family
that we had killed and covered up–

later that night
when I would see my father again
back in Popple Creek
wiping his plate with a piece of bread.

IN THE HO BO WOODS

She took two rounds
before going down like a small doe.

When she hit the hard ground,
the bamboo basket on her back jarred open.

Like little comrades going for help,
three brown hens went screeching off.

Hippo came running through the elephant grass
to wrap her seeping body with layers of gauze.

Papa Bear ordered me to carry her
to a clearing by the river.

Harlem Hare took my rucksack,
then hoisted her onto me.

Feeling her warm body against my own,
I started to think of her in another way.

We all took on aliases that year.

STILL LIFE

His taut
brown body
erupted
in a hundred places
like
butterscotch pudding
coming to a boil.

Then
he lay still

as we slithered
back
into the rainforest.

THESE HANDS

These hands
clutching
the blood and betel-stained Mauser
were good hands.

And while he lay
forever silent now,
these thick
and tethered-to-earth hands
yet spoke,

suggesting–
            no,
insisting–

we would have liked
one another.

"So that wondrous sadness may live forever,
you've been turned into my memory."

Anna Akhmatova

I AM THINKING

I am thinking
   of your entrance from the woodline,
   the gait of a farm boy
   with his chores half done.

I am thinking
   that because you were the tallest and strongest,
   that they gave you the machine gun to carry.

I am thinking
   that whatever your nickname was,
   it could be traced to the manure on your sandals.

I am thinking
   that on that morning you were not alone,
   that along with those you loved
   were all those who loved you.

I am thinking
   but that I saw you first–
   we were equal.

THE DARK FOREST

Fueled
by
Myth and Fear
we
advanced
deep
into
the dark forest
leaving
orphans
in
our wake
like bread crumbs
that
we might find
our
way
back again
to
innocence.

Written after visiting orphanage at Kontum.

LITTLE FOLKS

Today,
I saw little folks,
eyes running over with yesterday,

little folks,
with state-of-the-art scars
behind little doors
all bolted
from the inside now.

Today,
I saw little folks,
eyes running over with yesterday,
and wondered
of their tomorrows.

ONCE JESUS HAD A CLEFT PALATE

As "number one shoe-shine boy"
snuggled closer
under "numbah one G.I.'s" poncho,

"numbah one G.I." wondered:

who was this little guy
and what right had he to tug
in places long hardened over
like a winter pond?

IT AIN'T GOOD,
WHAT WE DONE

Still hitched
to the primitive plow,
the huge beast
looked down
in bovine awe
at the old man
mangled and moaning
in monsoon mud.

Later that night on guard
Tyus whispered;

"It ain't good, what we done."

THE GENERALS

Late at night,
in dim-lit tents
they stick pins
into voodoo maps.

Half-a-world away,
blood spurts out
in little places

like Willow Bend,
Cedar Falls and
Popple Creek.

"...My friend, you would not tell with such high zest, to children ardent for some desperate glory, the old lie: Dulce et Decorum est pro patria mori."

Wilfred Owen

"OH MOTHER"

As the small red flower
on Goulet's chest
turned to a bouquet

I heard
his last words–

and there was
in them
neither mention
of flag
nor of father

for there is
so little room
in a final breath.

Written after going through wallet
of enemy soldier at Tuy Hoa.

A THOUSAND WORDS OF HATE

A thousand
words of hate
employed
to dehumanize
and incite.

A thousand
words of hate
assigned
to replace kindness
with ruthlessness,
conscience with allegiance.

A thousand
words of hate
rendered false now
by one tattered telling photo
of a young man with girlfriend
(or maybe wife, I still wonder)
on a blue Vespa.

GONZALES

Gonzales had the
Lady of Guadalupe
tattooed on his chest.

Said it was his shield
and he'd be goin' home.

When we loaded him
onto the chopper,
he was smilin' so.

We had to believe
he was home now.

"God is my Pointman, Slackman, RTO, Medic and Ammo Bearer.
You know He's hard."

written on helmet at Kontum

OFTEN THEN

We called
on Him
often then.

We had
detoured bad;

no longer
would a
mere Triune God
suffice.

INTERUPTING A SONG
NEAR TUY HOA AT DUSK
in six parts

1. A nubile girl
   stooped over and singing
   in a shallow stream
   unwittingly washing the pots and pans
   of her last supper.

2. The beauty of her voice
   along with the nobility of her chore
   endeavor to inform us
   that we and our weapons
   are *out of place*.

3. It was by her black pajamas then
   that we came by our license.

4. Some dark minutes later
   her warm blood is following us
   posse-like downstream.

5. Harlem Hare radios Papa Bear:
        "Body Count– one
          Weapons– none."

6. Not until morning
   would we notice our dyed boots–

            an adamant color–
            with half a song still in it.

"SNIPS AND SNAILS
AND PUPPY DOG TAILS"

Seven
school-bound boys
opened
claymore wide–

seven
school-bound boys
spread thin
like strawberry jam
onto a slice
of Asian meadow.

Seven
school-bound boys
opened claymore wide
revealing now–
how all had lied.

Everyone had lied–

even his mother.

MEKONG GALLERY

In the soft brown skin
between her shoulder blades
were three small holes–

like someone had meant
to hang her on their wall
and had trouble finding
dead center.

HOLY TIME

"Hold your fire"
was followed
by Holy Time in Nam.

Holy Time
when the wounded
could be heard
imploring
their respective gods
in gargled tones.

Holy Time
when the dead
were poncho-wrapped
and laid side-by-side
like giant cucumbers
in a great garden.

Holy Time
when those still whole
would tremble
and ponder–

what if?

MOSTLY I REMEMBER UMBERTO

I remember Umberto,
   how reluctant he was in the rain
   to maintain his weapon.

I remember Umberto,
   with the black book of Psalms
   next to his grenades.

I remember Umberto,
   how he would sprinkle Holy Water
   onto the bodies of both sides.

I remember Umberto,
   conflicted
   like a nun wearing lipstick.

Mostly I remember Umberto–
   the children swarming around him
   as if somehow they knew
   his weapon had rusted up.

PAPPY

Lured by a Screaming Eagle,
Silver Wings,
and an ambiguous cause,
you went off
certain of your charge–

rolled along by fate
and an olive drab myth,
only to find youth
your true adversary.

Silenced in the end
by a faceless foe,
you left us saddened
and asking– why?

BORN 4 JULY 1947
DIED 3 MARCH 1967

remembering
David C. Papesh
(Pappy)

You ask:

"How beautiful is war?"
and I say:

"Beautiful enough
to take
a young man's
breath away."

GOD, HE MUST BE SAD

At a side altar
in a dark crypt
she lights a candle;
then prays hard that
her soldier-son might live.

In order that
her soldier-son might live,
he must kill others.

Others,
whose mothers light candles
and pray hard that
their soldier-sons might live.

God, He must be sad.

TELL ME AGAIN

Tell me, how is it you want
your Star-Spangled truth served;

easy over like the old peasant
mangled and moaning in monsoon mud
because his small bundle of bamboo
"looked like a weapon from where we were,"

sunny-side up like the little napalmed girl,
her breasts sizzling on her chest
like two banty eggs,

or *well done* like the seven school-bound boys
opened claymore wide and spread thin
like strawberry jam onto a slice of Asian meadow?

Tell me again, how is it you want
your Star-Spangled truth served?

ON BELONGING

To a Squad
   a Platoon
   a Company
To a Battalion
   a Division
   an Army
We were cloaked
rag-lady deep in belonging then.

We had come from different places
to bond under Georgia sun
on Dying Cockroaches and Jody chant.

From different places
to pull mental slack,
that is, to grow in such a way
so that later there would always
be someone nearby to say:
   "You did the right thing."
   "I would have done the same thing."
   "Anyone would have done the same thing."

Later
the layers of belonging
fell like veils in a Bedouin tent
and we stood naked and alone.

Naked and alone
we went back to our different places.

Part III

He asked: "What are you playing there? It sounds like all the world's dark sorrows rolled in one."

The Tale of Kieu

Nguyen Du

THE FRAGMENTS
OF WAR

By far
the soldier's memoir
is the easiest to assemble,

for his memories
are burr-like

and can be found
all in the same dark place
clinging to the burden.

ON FINDING ANNE FRANK
IN THE HO BO WOODS

Tonight
in the Blue Eagle Bar
in Sauk Rapids, Minnesota
the talk was of war–

war they surmised
was like a shoe
that comes
in different styles and sizes:

the earlier one of Hitler–
an engineer's boot,
the latter of Ho–
a mere sandal.

I had need
to tell them then
of how it is that war
only comes in one style
and in one size–

the style and size
of one man's breath.

TWO LANGUAGES

The two
languages of war
are Life and Death,
and every soldier
is fluent in both:

two languages
that can only be spoken
at the same time,
like our fathers did
German and English
in the same sentence,

two languages
at the same time,
for in war
it is not possible
to speak Life
without having spoken
Death.

RECALLING NOW

Recalling now:

the killing of the chickens,
the burning of the granary,
the smashing of his plow–

Recalling now:

the breaking of the harrow,
the killing of the sow,
the taking of his seed–

Recalling now:

Emslander, Spirowski,
Schreifels and I–
we farm boys, at least
should have known better.

PLOWING AROUND THE
SANDPIPER'S NEST

a gold star mother remembers

Paul's mother loves to recall,
how her husband gave their son hell
for plowing around the cluster
of small speckled eggs.

She likes to recall, how the following year
in an adjacent field, Paul bartered once again
to go around the small eggs
in exchange for the wrath of his father.

This memory of her son on the Farmall tractor
with the three bottom Oliver plow in tow–

this memory of her Paul going out of his way
with God's small creatures in mind–

this memory is the only one
muscular enough to carry her now
out of the darkness and into tomorrow–

this memory of her Paul
plowing around the sandpiper's nest.

CHIEF

for Glenn Good Thunder

Many moons ago
in a distant land
of pannier and pagoda,
he left footprints.

Now the Great Spirit
tracks him
like a wounded elk
in fresh winter snow.

BEASLEY

the red, white and blue

I knew Beasley in his youth–
a youth that was like
a scale out of balance.

Along with his gear
Beasley left an Amerasian daughter
with beautiful red hair and blue eyes
in his wake.

Beasley's last memory
of his daughters' mother
has her laying on a straw mat
with tears running toward her ears.

Today after five decades
I went back to Nam
with *Black is Black* by Los Bravos.

Tonight I got down on my knees
and prayed for Beasley–

prayed that if and when
it finally weighed on him
it was not more than he could carry.

BERNARD

He had duct-taped
her best paring knife
to the barrel
of his BB gun.

From an upstairs window
she watched
as he gleefully stabbed
the small red sparrow
again and again.

Years later,
when the taller soldier
handed her the telegram,
she tried to recall
when it was
he really died.

GOOD CONDUCT

On the eve
following the birth
of his first son,
Elmer went up-garret
to study his medals;

leaned over them
like a monk would
an ancient scroll
in quest of answers

and could find
no cause for quarrel,
when in front
of his moist eyes
they turned
to Commandments–

some broken–

all bent.

NO PAYMENTS TILL APRIL

One side of his helmet read:
"Avoid Jetlag: Go Body Bag,"
the other: "Death Spoken Here."
We skirted him
like a farmer would a slough-hole.
    Wrecking Ball was hard,
    wrecking ball hard.

Two tours on the line.
Ask anybody and they'll tell you:
guys who put two tours on the line
were fewer than vegetarians
who pray the rosary.

Back home,
he never talked Nam.
Not even his Ma noticed
when he stopped using
the future tense.
    Wrecking Ball was hard,
    wrecking ball hard.

It was late October
when his Pa found him
hanging in the box elder grove
behind the granary

and wondered…

who would do the spring plowing?

TWO CARPENTERS

Because he could remember
taking his turn with a crossbow
shooting arrows into a black sow
while blood dripped
onto her piglets below–

because he could remember
holding a naked Montagnard girl
while dreams drained
from a small hole behind her ear–

because he could remember
removing a Nazi-issue Lugar
from the warm hand
of a North Vietnamese Colonel–

because he could remember
these things, and more,
he took the time each night
to tell his two sons
the stories of an earlier Carpenter.

Because he could remember
he cried
when in the fresh scraps of pine
that fell at the feet of his sawhorses
they found for themselves–
one, a rifle;
the other, a pistol–

then disappeared into the woodline.

IN A BAD PLACE

The chaplain said,
"This will do,"
then commenced to lay
a camouflaged cloth
over a pallet
stacked with mortar rounds.

In olive-drab ponchos
we stood round
our new-found altar,
like an order of monks
that had detoured
in a terrible way.

Ankle deep in red mud
we prayed
the same skinny prayers
that have always gone up
from those who find themselves
in a bad place.

Forty years later I wonder:
what does God do with such prayers,
the prayers of those He knows
at dawn will follow their altar
into the valley below?

THE FRAGILITY OF BRAVADO

remembering Paul Wittenburg

Wittenburg said
he hoped to be assigned to
a "Demoralization Squad."

I asked him then
what that was
and he explained–

"Soldiers trained
to slip into the enemies camp
under darkness—slit
every second man's throat
while they were asleep
and then to leave undetected."

Thirteen months later
I met Wittenburg again
at the Army hospital
in Yokohama, Japan

where I shook his shaking hand.

FLOOD PLAIN

for Jim Kaufman

Day after day,
year after year,

with sand
from a dark time,

he fills the small
olive drab bags,

then stacks them
around himself,

uncertain–

on which side
the water will rise.

AN ELUSIVE DEROS

Elmer told them
about the gray
squirrel throwing
the grenade.

They laughed
so darned hard
at him then.

He will not
tell them about
the woodchuck
in black pajamas.

DEROS: Date of Expected Return from Overseas

YOU SAID GOD WAS ON OUR SIDE

You said God was on our side; I was there and did
not see Him. Which one was He?

Was He the one that triggered the ambush killing
the seven young boys on their way to school?

Was He the one that raped the already wounded
woman prisoner near Phan Rang?

Was He the one that shot the panniered old man
crossing a rice paddy, just to sight his weapon in?

Was He the one that set fire to the Montagnard
granaries in the Highlands?

Was He the one that dropped the napalm from
twenty thousand feet onto the peasants below?

Was He the one that blew the water buffalo into
the side of a mountain with an anti-tank weapon
"just to have some fun?"

Was He the one strutting with a Viet Cong ear
floating in a vial tied to his lapel?

You said God was on our side; I was there and did
not see Him. Which one was He?

TOUR OF DUTY

Of him already
on his way to hell
I have no qualm
with tour,

but of the other:
the one who was
on his way to heaven,

would not honesty
be better served
by detour?

ELMER MEETS PONTIUS PILATE
IN THE SHADOW OF
THE FIRST AMERICAN BANK

(Mathew 27:24)

You must trust me when I say
that you know too little of my service
to ever thank me for it.

You must come to see how it is
that I find your gratitude more odorous
than I would your scorn.

You must trust me when I inform you
that along with all of the slogans,
I have sliced and diced my service
into pieces the size of orphans–

that I have studied the pieces
under the light that only time can afford–

and you must trust me too
when I tell you I found nothing there
that either you or I could ever use
to wash our hands.

WHEN I HEAR SOUVENIR

When I hear souvenir
my mind goes to a swaggering corporal,
a darkening sky and monsoon mud.

When I hear souvenir
an old man's gold tooth comes into view
along with the bayonet
used to pry it from his still warm jaw.

When I hear souvenir
I think of a world out of order,
and the gruesome dentistry of war.

When I hear souvenir
the loquacious kind comes to mind–
the kind that goes on ad nauseam
from the mantle in the living room
at eye level–

the kind assigned
to provide quarter for bravado,
mendacity and masculine madness–

the kind aware of how crucial it is
to keep alive the myth.

PAPPY II

They are saying
you were brave, Pappy,
that what we did was good.
When I say
you were not brave, Pappy,
that what we did was not good,
they do not understand.

But you understand,
don't you, Pappy?

If I let them say
you were brave,
that what we did was good,
they will use
their memory of you
to kill again and again.

That is why
I cannot let them say
you were brave,
that what we did was good.
Don't you see, Pappy?
I can find no other way
to give meaning to your death.

DOUBLE VISION

Five decades
has brought him
to this place,

this place
that informs him
he no longer is
who he once was,

but this place
has no sanctuary in it,

for in his mind
close behind
it followed then,

not only had he killed
who they were
but, too,
who they were to become.

WAR ZONE

Do you ever want to go back they ask
and always what they mean is
back to a place and not a time.

What they do not understand is
that Time as we know it
was the runt of the litter–
a runt resigned forever to schlep around
remorse and regret, lament and sorrow.

What they do not understand is
that what is called for now
is a more hearty variety of Time:

one able to put the warmth
back into the body
of a little Montagnard girl–

one that could fill a house
with the laughter of her grandchildren–

one that would flourish in every zone.

FOOTNOTE

Every soldier's prayer
is the same:
that God will see
the uniform
and then commence
to set aside the norm;

that He will know
where it is we stood,
and then choose
to place an asterisk
beside the blood.

Photo by Don Hoffmann.

J. Vincent Hansen grew up on a farm east of Sauk Rapids, Minnesota. After High School, he served in Viet Nam (1966-67) as a machine gunner with the 101st Airborne Division. Following his time in the army, he spent seven years working in East Africa as an agricultural volunteer with the Maryknoll Fathers.

In addition to the books *Blessed Are the Piecemakers*, *Without Dividend in Mind,* and *The Medicine of Place*, he is the author of the multi-media play *The Wedding of Tomorrow and Sorrow*. He lives with his wife, Jeanette, in Sauk Rapids, Minnesota.

Dick Adair (1935-2018) was a Navy Journalist and War Correspondent for the military newspaper *Stars and Stripes* and also the author of the book *Saigon* published by Weatherhill 1971. Later in life, his art brought him many awards while working as a cartoonist in Honolulu, Hawaii.

It was only after coming upon Dick's deceptively simple line drawings that I came to see the complimentary nature of our work and I shall always be thankful to Margot Adair for her willingness to bring this collaboration forward.

JVH